LIONS

A TRUE BOOK®

by

Ann O. Squire

Children's Press®
A Division of Scholastic Inc.

New York Toronto London Auckland Sydney
Mexico City New Delhi Hong Kong
Danbury, Connecticut

A lion carrying her cub

Reading Consultant
Nanci R. Vargus, Ed.D.
Assistant Professor,
School of Education,
University of Indianapolis

Content Consultant
Kathy Carlstead, Ph.D.
Research Scientist,
Honolulu Zoo

Dedication:
For Emma

Library of Congress Cataloging-in-Publication Data

Squire, Ann.
    Lions / by Ann O. Squire.
        p. cm. — (A True book)
    Summary: Describes the physical characteristics, habitats, and behavior
of lions.
    Includes bibliographical references (p.   ).
    ISBN 0-516-22795-5 (lib. bdg.)   0-516-27936-X (pbk.)
    1. Lions—Juvenile literature. [1. Lions.] I. Title. II. Series.
QL737.C23S64 2003
599.757—dc21

2003005172

1 2 3 4 5 6 7 8 9 10 R 14 13 12 11 10 09 08 07 06 05

Contents

A male African lion

The King of Beasts

There once lived a king whose bravery in battle earned him the name Richard the Lion Hearted. Expressions like "lion-hearted," "strong as a lion," and "brave as a lion" have long been used to describe people who are courageous, loyal, and strong. It's no surprise, then,

Male lions are slightly larger than female lions.

that the lion is considered the king of beasts.

The lion may be king, but it is not the largest of the big cats. That honor goes to the tiger. Female lions generally weigh about 300 pounds (136 kilograms), while males can tip the scales at over 400 pounds (181 kg). Some really huge males may reach 500 pounds (227 kg).

Lions once roamed across the Middle East, India, and much of Africa. Unfortunately, these big cats have always been favorite **prey** for hunters. Over the years, thousands of lions have been killed for sport. In many places, the **savannas** where lions live have been turned into farms or ranches, and the lions have been killed or forced to find other homes.

Lions and elephants living on a wildlife preserve in East Africa

Today, about 50,000 to 100,000 wild lions live in **wildlife preserves** south of the Sahara Desert in Africa. About 200 lions live in India's Gir Forest. These Asiatic lions are among the world's most **endangered** cats.

Even in protected areas, life is not easy for lions. In the wild, they usually live 15 to 18 years. In **captivity**, however, where they do not need to fight or hunt for food, lions can live for 25 years or longer.

The few lions still left in Asia live in the Gir Forest of India.

A Most Unusual Cat

The lion is a very different creature from the house cat that may be sitting on your lap right now. Not only is a lion a lot bigger than a **domestic** cat, it can do something that smaller cats cannot. A lion can roar. In fact, lions make the loudest sound of any cat, big

or small. A lion's roar can be heard as far away as 5 miles (8 kilometers)!

Lions are not just different from their smaller relatives, but from other big cats, as well. Most cats prefer to live

and hunt alone, getting together only for mating. Lions, on the other hand, are very social. They live together in groups called prides.

A pride consists of several relat-ed females and their cubs, plus at least two to four adult males. When the cubs grow up, some of the young females stay in the pride with their mother, aunts, and sisters. Other females leave to form their own prides. All the young males leave when they are about three years old. They

A young male lion leaves its pride and goes out on its own when it is about three years old.

wander around looking for a new pride to join. A pride usually has about fifteen members, but it can have as few as four lions or as many as forty.

Lions are the only members of the cat family whose males and females do not look alike. In addition to being bigger than the female, the male lion has an impressive mane that makes him look even larger than he actually is. The male's main job is to defend the

pride's territory and protect
the females against **intruders**,
so it helps to look as big and
scary as possible. Without his
showy mane, the male lion
would be just another cat.

Life in the Pride

Why do lions live in prides? Even if you travel to Africa to observe wild lions, the answer won't be obvious right away. Like other cats, lions spend most of their time sleeping. If you watch for long enough, however, you'll begin to see that different pride members have different jobs.

Lions spend a huge amount of their time sleeping.

Two female lions
with their cubs

For example, females have
the job of raising the cubs.
Also, when night falls, it is the
females that go out hunting.

On the Prowl.

Lions hunt mainly at night, and their excellent vision and hearing help them to locate their prey. Once they spot a prey animal, lions creep as close as possible and then chase or pounce on their victim. Did you know that a lion can travel 35 feet (10.7 meters) in one giant jump?

A female lion hunting wildebeest

Like other cats, lions are car-
nivores, or meat eaters. Working
together, several lionesses can
bring down prey as large as a
zebra or wildebeest.

Even though the females do most of the work of hunting, it is the males in the pride that get to eat first. This is not

Adult males, the strongest members of the pride, always are first in line at mealtime.

After the males are done, the females and cubs get their turn.

because the females are generous. It is because the males are so large and strong that they can easily steal whatever the females have brought back. After **gorging** themselves on as much as 75 pounds (34 kg) of meat apiece, the males allow the females and cubs to eat whatever is left.

While the females hunt and raise the young, the males defend the pride and its territory against intruders. You may wonder what kind of animal would attack a pride of lions. The answer is other lions.

Male lions fighting

Many young male lions are not members of prides. These lions are always on the lookout for a pride to join. When they come upon a pride whose males seem old or weak, they attack and try to drive the pride males away. If they are successful, the new males take over the pride and its females. The **defeated** males must go off on their own.

Raising Cubs

Although lions are very sociable cats, there are times when they prefer to be alone. One of these times is when cubs are born. Before giving birth, the lioness leaves the pride and finds a safe hiding place, usually in thick bushes or a wooded

Lion cubs are blind and helpless at birth.

area. Then she gives birth to a litter of two to five tiny, helpless cubs.

At birth, the cubs are blind and can barely crawl, so it is

When lion cubs are very young, their mother keeps them well hidden.

no wonder that their mother keeps them safely hidden. For several weeks, she cares for the cubs, leaving them only to find food or water for herself. Yet even for hidden cubs, the world is a dangerous place. Each time the lioness leaves her cubs, there is a chance that they will be captured and killed by hyenas, jackals, or other **predators**.

By ten to twelve weeks, the cubs can begin to follow their mother. Now she is able to lead them from their hiding place and introduce them to the rest of the pride. The female lions in a pride often have their cubs at about the

When cubs are a few months old, they are brought out to join the rest of the pride.

same time, so the chances are good that the cubs will have some playmates about their own age.

After joining the pride, the cubs learn something new

every day. By following their mother on hunting expeditions, they learn the skills they will need to stalk and capture prey. By playing with each other and

Lion cubs play-fighting with each other

with adult lions, they learn the rules of the pride. By wrestling and pouncing on one another, they learn the fighting techniques they will need to defend their territories.

When they are a bit over a year old, the cubs lose their baby teeth. These are replaced by the large, sharp canine teeth they will need to kill prey. Now the cubs can begin to take part in hunts and practice the skills they have been

As they get older, the cubs begin to join the adult lions on hunts.

learning. In another few months, their mother will stop caring for them and bringing them food. At this point, the young lions will hunt on their own.

How Lions Communicate

Like humans and other animals that live in groups, lions have many different ways of communicating. Touch, smell, sight, and sound all play a part in lion communication.

When two pride members meet, they rub their heads together. This greeting

These two male lions, who are probably brothers, are greeting each other.

serves the same purpose as a human handshake or hug—it shows that both animals are friendly and mean no harm.

The sense of smell is also important in lion communication. When a male lion wants to mark the edges of his pride's territory, he sprays a mixture of urine and his own special scent on shrubs and trees. Another lion passing by can smell the scent marks. They tell him that the territory belongs to someone else. Lions also use scent signals to locate other members of their pride and

A male lion marking its territory

to help **distinguish** pride members from strange lions.

Lions have excellent vision. So it's not surprising that they use body postures and facial expressions to communicate. One of the most obvious signals is the male lion's large mane. It says "I am a big, strong male. Don't mess with me!" To send this signal even more clearly, the lion will sometimes strut back and forth with his head and tail held high.

A lion with its tail up means
"Don't mess with me!"

A female lion baring her teeth and flattening her ears

Lions also show their feelings by staring, **baring** their teeth, or flattening their ears.

Lions are probably best known for their loud roars. Lions roar as a way of announcing their territory, and also to find pride members that may be far away. Lions also hiss, growl,

A male lion growling

What do you think this mother is saying to her cubs?

snarl, and meow. Some of these sounds are not too different from those made by domestic cats, and the meanings are often the same. The next time you visit the zoo, spend a few minutes watching the lions. It may be easier than you think to figure out what they're saying to one another.

To Find Out More

Here are some additional resources to help you learn more about lions:

 **Books**

Barnes, Julia. **101 Facts About Lions.** Gareth Stevens, 2004.

Klevansk, Rhonda. **Nature Watch: Big Cats** (Nature Watch Series), Lorenz Books, 1997.

Markle, Sandra. **Outside and Inside Big Cats.** Atheneum, 2003.

Winner, Cherie. **Lions** (Our Wild World). Northward Press, 2001.

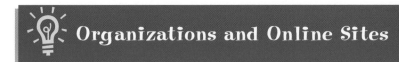

Organizations and Online Sites

African Savannah: African Lion
http://www.oaklandzoo.org/ atoz/azlion.html

You can hear a lion roar at this site sponsored by the Oakland Zoo.

The Cyber Zoomobile: Lions
http://home.globalcrossing. net/~brendel/lion.html

This site is packed with information about the habitat, behavior, and life cycle of lions.

The Lion Research Center
http://www.lionresearch.org/

This site, from the University of Minnesota, includes lots of lion facts and information about lion conservation projects.

Asiatic Lion Information Centre
http://www.asiatic-lion.org/

This site includes facts about this highly endangered lion subspecies as well as infor-mation on conservation.

Important Words

baring showing, revealing

captivity being under the care and protection of humans

defeated one who has lost a battle

distinguish to tell the difference between

domestic describing animals that are no longer wild and that are kept as work animals or pets

endangered in danger of disappearing

gorging stuffing oneself with food

intruders unwanted outsiders

predators animals that hunt other animals

prey animal hunted by other animals or by humans

savannas grassy plains with few trees

wildlife preserves areas set aside so that animals can live safely in their natural habitats

Index

Meet the Author

Ann O. Squire has a Ph.D. in animal behavior. Before becoming a writer, she spent several years studying African electric fish and the special signals they use to communicate with each other. Dr. Squire is the author of many books on animals and natural science topics, including *African Animals, Animal Homes, Cheetahs,* and *Jaguars.* She and her children, Emma and Evan, share their home with a not-so-wild cat named Isabel.